SHAKTI GITA

Twameva Māta Cha Pitā Twameva
Twameva Bandhu Cha Sakha Twameva
Twameva Vidya Dravinum Twameva
Twameva Sarvam Mum Deva Deva

You are my mother and father as well.
You are my family and friends as well.
You are my wisdom and wealth as well.
You are everything, O god of the gods!

INTRODUCTION

The scholars have struggled to understand 'Hinduism', a faith whose followers seemed to be crazy because they worshipped a large number of gods and goddesses as the supreme. A religion vastly diverse in its beliefs, practices and the ways of worship. Some labelled hinduism as polytheistic while others even coined new terms, like henotheism, to describe this baffling array of spiritual traditions. Few, however, have realised, and fewer still have written, that 'Sanatana Dharma' or the eternal faith known today as hinduism and comprising nearly a billion followers, is a family of religions with four principal sects namely; 'Shaktism', 'Shaivism', 'Vaishnavism' and 'Smartism'. This single perception is very essential for understanding hinduism and explaining it accurately.

Contrary to prevailing misconceptions, we must know that hindus worship one supreme deity, though by different names. For Vaishnavite, Lord Vishnu is the supreme. For Shaivite, Lord Shiva is the supreme. For Shakta, Mother Shakti is the supreme. For Smarta, the liberal hindus, the choice of deity is left to the devotee.

Each has a multitude of guru lineages, religious leaders, sacred literatures, monastic communities, pilgrimage centres and a number of temples. They possess a huge wealth of art, architecture and philosophy. These four sects hold such divergent beliefs that each is a complete and independent religion in itself. Yet, they share a vast heritage of culture and common beliefs; reincarnation, temple-worship, manifold deities, the guru-shishya tradition and the Vedas as their scriptural authority.

Each of philosophies, schools and lineages shares a common purpose to enhance the soul's journey towards purity and perfection known as 'Moksha' or liberation. Let's discuss all the sects one by one.

Shaktism

Shaktas worship the supreme as the divine mother, Shakti or Devi. The supreme mother has many forms. Some are gentle and others are fierce. Shaktas use chanting, holy diagrams, yoga and rituals to call forth cosmic forces and awaken the great kundalini power within the spine.

Shaivism

Shaivites worship the supreme as Lord Shiva, the auspicious one. Shaivites give utmost importance to self-discipline and philosophy. They worship in the temples and practice yoga, striving to be one with Shiva itself.

Vaishnavism

Vaishnavites worship the supreme as Lord Vishnu and incarnations, mostly Krishna and Rama. They are highly devotional. Their faith is rich in saints, scriptures and temples.

Smartism

Smartas worship all the major hindu gods and goddesses. Hence, they are also known as liberal hindus. They follow a philosophical, meditative path, emphasising our oneness with divinity through rational understanding.

CONTENTS

CHAPTER 01: BIRTH OF PARVATI
CHAPTER 02: KNOWLEDGE OF SHAKTI
CHAPTER 03: SHAKTI COSMIC FORM
CHAPTER 04: YOGA OF KNOWLEDGE
CHAPTER 05: YOGA AND MANTRA
CHAPTER 06: KNOWLEDGE OF SELF
CHAPTER 07: YOGA OF DEVOTION

Om Bhur Bhuvah Svah
Tat Savitur Varenyam
Bhargo Devasya Dhimahi
Dhiyo Yo Nah Prachodayat

The eternal self that creates the physical, the mental, and the spiritual world.
That source of all, I worship.
I meditate on that in the form of divine light.
May this light illuminate our intellect!

CHAPTER 01

BIRTH OF PARVATI

[1] King said: O Sage! You told me that the supreme light took birth on the top of the Himalayas. Now, describe in detail about this supreme light. No intelligent human can desist from hearing these nectar-like words about the divine mother.

[2] The danger of death may come even to the demigods drinking nectar but no such danger can possibly come to those who drink the nectar of the mother's glorious deeds.

[3] Sage said: O King! You are blessed that you have been taught by the greatest souls. You are so fortunate since you are sincerely devoted to Shakti.

[4] Now, hear the ancient tale when Shiva was wandering all over the world in a distracted state, carrying the Sati's body burnt by fire.

[5] Wherever Shiva rested, he spent time there with his senses controlled, forgetting all his knowledge of the world in a deep meditation of Shakti's forms.

[6] The three worlds with their objects, moving and unmoving, with oceans, mountains and islands became devoid of prosperity and power.

[7] Without any trace of joy, the hearts of all the embodied beings became dried up. They were all burdened with anxious thoughts and remained miserable.

[8] All beings were merged in the ocean of sorrow and became diseased. Planets moved in opposite directions and the demigods had lost their fortunes.

[9] The kings were attacked with a series of misfortunes, thus losing material and spiritual wealth. At this time a great demon, named Taraka, became unconquerable after receiving a boon from Brahma.

[10] Being intoxicated by his powers, he conquered the three worlds. The boon he received states that the legitimate son of Shiva only would be able to kill him.

[11] And as at that time Shiva had no son. Hence, the great demon, elated with joy, became infatuated with his powers.

[12] All the demigods were banished from their palaces by his oppression. They remained always anxious and fearful.

[13] Shiva has no wife now. How can he then have a son! We are very unfortunate. How can our work be accomplished?

[14] Thus, being oppressed with anxious thoughts, all the demigods went to 'Vaikuntha' and informed Vishnu of all that had happened.

[15] Vishnu said: Why are you all so anxious when the goddess of the universe, the yielder of all desires, is always wakeful for us.

[16] It is due to our faults that the divine mother is showing her disregard. It is meant to teach us and make us stronger.

[17] When a mother frightens and scolds a child, it is not that she has become merciless. So, the world mother, the controller of the universe will never be merciless to you regardless of your vices.

[18] A child commits offence or mistakes at every step. Who can tolerate that in these three worlds except the mother?

[19] Therefore, take refuge in the supreme mother, the goddess of the universe with sincere devotion. Shakti will certainly grant whatever you desire.

[20] Thus, after ordering the demigods, Vishnu with his consort Lakshmi and others went out to worship Devi.

[21] Going to the Himalayas, they soon engaged themselves in doing the act of worship.

[22] O King! Those who were well versed with the performance of sacrifice to the mother, began their sacrificial ceremonies and all started to take holy decisions.

[23] Thus, some devoted themselves to repeating numerous names of Shakti and singing hymns. Others are immersed in meditation of Shakti's forms.

[24] Some were committed to chanting mantras. Some were engaged in severe penances. Others were focused on mental sacrifices.

[25] Again, some began to worship the goddess of the universe without any sleep or rest by the seed mantra of 'Maya'. O King! Thus, several years passed.

[26] The ninth day of the month of 'Chaitra' on Friday, the supreme light of the greatest force suddenly appeared in front of them.

[27] That red light was equal to the crores of lightning streaks, and cool like the crores of moons. Again, the lustre was like the crores of suns combined. The Vedas personified were chanting hymns all around.

[28] That mass of fire was above, below, on all sides, in the middle and nowhere it was obstructed.

[29] The massive fire had no beginning, nor end. It was of the form of a divine light. The appearance was not that of male or female nor that of a hermaphrodite.

[30] O King! The demigods first closed their eyes in fright, but at the next moment, regaining some courage when they opened their eyes again, they beheld a wondrous sight.

[31] They found the highest light manifesting in the form of an exceedingly beautiful divine woman.

[32] Her youth was just blooming and her upraised breasts; fully rounded and noticeable, added to the beauty all around. Bracelets were on her hands, armlets on her four arms and necklace on her neck.

[33] The garland made of invaluable gems and jewels spread very bright lustre all around. Lovely ornaments on her waist making tinkling sounds and beautiful anklets were on her feet.

[34] The locks of hair flowing between her ears and cheek sparkled bright like the large black bees shining on the flower leaves of the blooming Ketaki flower. Her hips were nicely shaped and lovely. The line of hair over her navel gave additional beauty.

[35] Her lively lotus-face rendered more beautiful by the shining golden ear-ornaments; her mouth was filled with betel leaves mixed with camphor.

[36] On her forehead, there was the half crescent moon. Her eyebrows were extended and her eyes looked bright and splendid like the red lotus. Her nose was elevated and her lips were very sweet.

[37] Her teeth were very beautiful like the opening buds of Kunda flowers. From her neck was suspended a necklace of pearls and on her head was the brilliant crown decked with diamonds and jewels. On her ears, earrings were suspended like the lines on the moon.

[38] Her hair was ornamented with Mallika and Malati flowers. Her forehead was pasted with Kashmiri saffron drops and her three eyes were shining in a playful mood.

[39] On her one hand there was the noose and on her other hand there was the goad. Her two other hands made signs granting boons and dispelling fears. Her body shed lustre like the flowers of a Darima tree. Her clothing is red coloured. All these added great beauty.

[40] The mother of the whole universe, the enchantress of all, very sweet, ever smiling, yielding all desires, worshipped by all the demigods and indicative of all lovely feelings.

[41] Thus, the demigods saw before them the mother goddess, the incarnate of unpretended mercy, with a face ready to offer her grace. The demigods bowed as soon as they saw her.

[42] Seeing that form of mother filled with compassion. All the demigods choked with emotion, unable to speak, shed tears in silence with their heads bent low.

[43] Having somehow controlled themselves, they began to chant hymns to the mother of the world with eyes filled with tears of love and devotion.

[44] Demigods said: Salutations to you, the great goddess! We bow down to you, the auspicious one. Our eternal salutations!

[45] You reside as a red flame in the heart of a yogi and worshipped by the demigods and all the 'Jivas' or individual souls for the rewards of their actions. Burning with asceticism and wisdom, shining everywhere as the pure consciousness, we take refuge in the goddess Durga. O Mother! We bow down to you, help us in crossing this terrible ocean of world.

[46] We have created the words and the language so that we can praise and chant hymns to you. You are like Kāma Dhenu (the heavenly cow yielding all desires) who nourishes the whole world. O Mother! Be pleased with us.

[47] O Devi! You are the night of destruction at the end of the world, praised by Brahma. You are Lakshmi, the shakti of Vishnu. You are the mother of Skanda and the shakti of Shiva. You are Sarasvati, the shakti of Brahma. You are Aditi, the mother of all the demigods. You are Sati, the daughter of Daksha. Thus, you purify the worlds in various forms and give peace to all. We bow down to you.

[48] We know you to be Maha Lakshmi. We meditate on you as the power of all beings. O Bhagavati! Illumine us so that we can progress in our wisdom and know you.

[49] O Shakti! Salutations to your gross cosmic form. To the subtle form that threads all, our salutation! Salutations to your unmanifested form. You are the embodiment of eternal self.

[50] Your ignorance causes delusion in humans. You are the maya under whose influence this whole world is created.

[51] You are the essence of consciousness. You are the eternal bliss, whom the Vedas describe as one's sole purpose in life. We bow down again and again to your lotus feet.

[52] We bow down to the one who is beyond the five bodily sheaths (Physical, Energy, Mental, Wisdom and Bliss). One who is witness to the three states (Wakefulness, Dream and Sleep). One who resides in all beings in the form of an individual soul.

[53] O Mother! You are Pranava 'Om' in all the mantras, also you are the 'Hrim' seed mantra. You are the most merciful and compassionate.

[54] Thus, praised by the demigods. Bhagavati spoke in a very sweet voice resembling a joyous Cuckoo.

[55] Goddess said: O Wise Ones! What do you want? I am yours, always ready to grant boons to my devotees.

[56] You are my devotees. Then, why do you care when I am on your side? I will rescue you from the ocean of troubles and set you free. Know my words to be true.

[57] Hearing these words of deep love, the demigods became very glad and their minds were put to rest.

[58] Demigods said: O Devi! You are omniscient and witness to all the worlds. What is there in the three worlds that is not known to you!

[59] O Mother! The lord of all the demons, Taraka is giving us troubles day and night.

[60] Brahma has given him the boon that he will be killed by Shiva's son only. Also, Sati, the wife of Shiva has cast aside her body. Hence, Shiva doesn't have a companion now.

[61] What will the ignorant people tell the one who is omniscient? O Mother! We have described in brief all that we could say. What more shall we say? You know all our troubles and the causes of our sorrow.

[62] Bless us so that our devotion remains unflinching at your lotus feet, this is our earnest prayer. O Mother! You assume a body to have a son of Shiva is our fervent prayer.

[63] After hearing the demigod's plight, Devi said: My shakti will soon incarnate as Parvati in the house of the mountain king, Himavan.

[64] She will be the wife of Shiva and will beget a son that will destroy Taraka demon and will serve your purpose. And your devotion will remain steadfast at my lotus feet.

[65] King Himavan with complete devotion worships me in his heart. Therefore, it gives me immense pleasure to take birth in his house without doubt.

[66] Sage said: O King! Hearing the kind words of the divine mother, the king of mountains was filled with love, and with a voice choked with feelings and with tears in his eyes spoke to the goddess of the three worlds.

[67] Himavan said: On whom you shower grace, you make them greater. Otherwise, I am so dull and unworthy, whereas you are the pure consciousness of the nature of existence, intelligence and bliss.

[68] O Sinless One! My becoming your father after crores of births is not possible without your grace. Even with the merits of penances and meditations combined.

[69] Oh! What a favour you have done towards me! Henceforth, my fame will spread throughout the universe that 'The world mother is born as daughter to Himavan'.

[70] One whose belly contains millions of universes, she herself should be my daughter. Who can be so blessed and fortunate on this earth!

[71] In whose family exists a blessed person like me, my ancestors had accumulated so much merits. I cannot imagine those heavenly realms created for my ancestors to dwell!

[72] O Mother! You are the goal of all Vedanta. Now describe to me your real self as exemplified in all the Vedas so that by that knowledge I will be able to realise the true self.

[73] The path of knowledge and devotion are approved by the scriptures. Hence, O Supreme Ruler! Please tell me how I may finally merge with you.

[74] Sage said: O King! Thus, hearing the praise of Himavan, the goddess of the universe gracefully began to reveal the secrets which are concealed in the authentic scriptures.

CHAPTER 02

KNOWLEDGE OF SHAKTI

[1] Devi said: O Immortals! Hear my words with attention and devotion, that I am now going to speak to you, hearing which will enable you to realise my true essence.

[2] Before the creation, I, only I existed, nothing else was existent then. My real self is called pure consciousness.

[3] My true self is beyond thought, beyond any name, without any comparison, beyond birth, beyond death or any other change. My self has one inherent power called maya.

[4] This maya is not existent, nor non-existent, nor can it be called both. This unspeakable substance always exists till the final liberation is achieved.

[5] Maya naturally arises from me as the heat comes out of fire, the hot light comes out of the sun and the cool light comes out of the moon.

[6] Just as all the actions of the beings dissolve in deep sleep, so at the time of dissolution, the actions of the beings, the beings and time itself all become merged in this great maya.

[7] I am the cause of this world. The maya, also my shakti, has the ability to hide me, its originator.

[8] I am formless. But, when I am united with my shakti, maya, I take various forms, the great cause of this world. This maya is divided into two; knowledge and ignorance. Knowledge liberates whereas ignorance hides me and thus creates bondage and suffering for beings.

[9] Maya united with five elements is the material cause of the universe. Some call her inert material; some call her ignorance. Others call her nature and energy.

[10] Maya is called the reasoning power by those who have proficiency in Shaiva-texts. Whereas, those who delve deep in Vedic principles called it an illusion.

[11] That which is seen is inert, for this reason, maya is inert and tangible. Also, the knowledge it conveys is destroyed in time, hence it is considered false.

[12] Consciousness cannot be perceived. If it were seen, it would have been inert. Pure consciousness is self-luminous not illumined by any other source.

[13] As a lamp is self-luminous and illuminates other objects, similarly consciousness illuminates what is other than itself. Hence, consciousness is self-luminous and it illuminates the sun, the moon, and other forms.

[14] O Himavan! Thus, my form of consciousness has been established as eternal and everlasting.

[15] The waking, dreaming and sleeping states do not remain constant but the sense of 'I' remains the same. Hence, the witness by which that absence of objects is felt in the sleeping state is eternal.

[16] Even if we suppose consciousness could be experienced, then by whom it would be experienced. That witness alone which experiences remains as pure consciousness.

[17] The saints have time and again declared that the consciousness is only eternal. It is the fountain of all love, the supreme love, the love beyond comparison.

[18] Jiva never feels 'I am not' but that 'I am' feeling is deeply established inside every being. Thus, it is clearly evident that I am quite separate from everything else. Also, I am one continuous flow of awareness without any intervals.

[19] I am therefore considered to be a complete and undivided whole. Consciousness is not an attribute of the self, since that would make an object of the self.

[20] Consciousness does not have attributes. Also, it is not separate from the self. Hence, consciousness is the self.

[21] Since, it is always unattached and devoid of duality. Therefore, its essence is bliss.

[22] The self, however by its own maya attaches to desires and actions, according to past tendencies.

[23] Maya is not separate from the self. Desirous to create, the entire world is created out of ignorance.

[24] The extraordinary form as described by me was an unmanifested form. It is the power of maya that brings creation to materialise.

[25] In all the scriptures, it is stated to be the cause of all the causes, of all the elements, it is the primaeval source. Its essence is existence, knowledge and bliss.

[26] Where all will power, intelligence and action, be melted in one, that is called the mantra 'Hrim'. It is the first principle of the universe.

[27] From this comes sky, having the property of sound, then air with touch property. And then comes fire with the property of form.

[28] Next arose water characterised by taste and lastly the earth having the quality of smell. Sound is the only attribute of sky, while air has two attributes; touch and sound.

[29] Fire has qualities of sound, touch and form. Whereas, water has sound, touch, form, and taste qualities.

[30] Earth has all five qualities; sound, touch, form, taste and smell. From these five elements, the subtle body is created.

[31] The subtle body that belongs to the self is all-pervading. When the subtle body is formed, that unmanifested form is called the causal body.

[32] The five elements being created, next by the five-fold grossification process, the gross elements are created. The process is now being explained.

[33] O Mountain King! Each of the five original elements is divided into two parts.

[34] One part of each of which is subdivided into four parts. This fourth part of each is united with the half of four other elements different from it and thus each gross element is formed. By these five elements, the gross body is formed.

[35] The gross body of the self is the result of a mixture of all the five elements in different proportions. The sense organs arise from the sattva guna of each of these five elements.

[36] The sattva gunas of each of the sense organs united become the internal organs. According to its functions, this is of four kinds.

[37] When it is engaged in willing or doubting, it is called mind. When it is free from doubts and when it arrives at the conclusion, it is called intellect.

[38] When it is engaged in recollection of memory, it is called 'Chitta'. Whereas when it identifies with the sense of 'I', it is called 'Ahankara' or the ego.

[39] From the rajas of each of the five elements arises speech, hands, feet, anus and genital organ. The five winds are formed when there is a combination of these aspects.

[40] Prana wind resides in the heart, Apana wind in the arms, Samana wind resides in the navel, Udana wind resides in the throat and Vyana wind resides pervading all over the body.

[41] My subtle body arises from the union of the five sense organs, the five organs of action, the five winds, the mind and the intellect, these seventeen elements.

[42] The Prakriti is divided into two parts; one is pure maya and the other is impure maya.

[43] The impure maya or ignorance is influenced by the three gunas. The pure maya or knowledge protects its devotees.

[44] When the supreme self is reflected on the pure maya, it is called Ishvara. This pure maya does not conceal the self.

[45] Therefore, she knows the all-pervading self and she is omniscient, omnipotent, and a blessing to all beings.

[46] When the supreme self is reflected on the impure maya or ignorance, it is called Jiva. This ignorance conceals the self whose nature is bliss. Therefore, this Jiva is the source of all miseries. Both Ishvara and Jiva have, by the influence of pure and impure maya, three bodies and three names.

[47] When the Jiva lives in the causal body, it is named Pragya, when it lives in the subtle body, it is known as Taijasa, while it has the gross body, it is called Vishva.

[48] When Ishvara is in the causal body, it is named Isha, when it is in the subtle body, it is known as Sutra, and when it is in the gross body, it is known as Virat.

[49] Ishvara is the lord of all and though it feels itself always happy and satisfied, yet to favour the Jivas and to give them liberation, it has created various sorts of worldly things for their enjoyment.

[50] The Ishvara creates all the universes, impelled by my power. It is conceived in me as a snake is imagined in a rope. Therefore, Ishvara has to remain dependent on my powers.

CHAPTER 03

SHAKTI COSMIC FORM

[1] Mother said: O Mountain King! This whole universe, moving and unmoving, is created by my power of maya. This maya in reality is not separate from me.

[2] There is no other knowledge than me. Viewed practically, maya is known as knowledge, but viewed from the point of soul, there is no such thing as maya, only one eternal self exists, I am that self, of the nature of knowledge.

[3] I create this whole world on this unchangeable eternal self and enter it as a vital breath.

[4] O King! Unless I enter as breath, how can this birth and death, leaving and retaking bodies be possible!

[5] As one great sky appears inside the pot as emptiness, so I too appear in various forms due to ignorance.

[6] As the sun rays are never defiled when they illuminate various objects on earth, so I too, am not defiled in entering into various high and low beings.

[7] The ignorant people attach intellect and other activities to me. The deluded say that the self acts, but this is not the thought of the wise. I remain as the witness in the hearts of all beings, not as the doer.

[8] As the one pervading sky is called Mahakasa, but being enclosed by jars, it is called Ghatakasa. Similarly, the one all-pervading Paramatma is called Jivatma being enclosed within the body.

[9] As the Jivas are conceived many by maya, but not in reality. So, the Ishvaras also are conceived many by maya, but not in essence.

[10] O Mountain King! This ignorance and nothing else is the cause of the difference in Jivas, by creating differences in their bodies, sense organs and minds.

[11] Again, due to the three gunas and their wants (Sattvik, Rajasik and Tamasik desires), maya also appears various.

[12] It is maya that differentiates between Brahma, Vishnu and Mahesha. O King! The whole world is interwoven in me.

[13] I am the subtle soul. Also, I am the gross cosmic body. I am Brahma, Vishnu and Rudra. Also, I am Brahmi, Vaishnavi and Gauri.

[14] I am the sun, I am the moon, I am the stars. I am the animals, birds, outcastes and also, I am the thief.

[15] I am the wicked one. Also, I am virtuous. I am the male, female and neuter as well. There is no doubt in this.

[16] O King! Wherever there is anything seen or heard, I always exist there as a witness, within and without.

[17] There is nothing moving or unmoving that can exist without me. Hence, I am everything indeed.

[18] Just as rope is mistaken for a snake, so I am the one who appears as Ishvara. There is no doubt in this.

[19] The world cannot appear without a substance. And that substance is me only. There can be nothing else.

[20] Himavan said: O Devi! If you are merciful to me, I wish to see your cosmic form.

[21] Sage said: Having heard his request, all the demigods rejoiced within their hearts and gladly praised Himavan.

[22] The auspicious one, knowing the desire of the demigods, showed her cosmic form that fulfils desires of the devotees.

[23] The Satyaloka is situated on the topmost part and is her head. Also, the sun and the moon are her eyes.

[24] The directions are her ears. The Vedas are her speech. The wind is her life breath. The universe is her heart. Also, the earth is her loins.

[25] The Bhuvarloka is her navel. The asterisms are her thighs. The Maharloka is her neck. The Janaloka is her face.

[26] Tapaloka is her forehead which is situated beneath the Satyaloka. Svargaloka are her arms. The sound is the organ of her ears.

[27] The Ashvini twins are her nose. The scent is the organ of smell. The fire is her mouth. And day and night are the lids of her eyes.

[28] The four-faced Brahma is her eyebrows. Water is her palate. Taste is her organ of tongue. The demigod of death is her fangs or large teeth.

[29] The affection is her small teeth. Maya is her smile. The creation of the universe is her side-looks. Modesty is her upper lip.

[30] Greed is her lower lip. Unrighteousness is her back. The Prajapati is her genital organ.

[31] The ocean is her belly. The mountains are her bones. The rivers are her veins, and the trees are the hairs of her body.

[32] O King! Childhood, youth and old age are her way of walking. The clouds are her hair. The thunder is her hair-locks. The two twilights are her clothing.

[33] The moon is the mind of the mother. Vishnu is her knowledge power and Rudra is her destroying power.

[34] The horses and other animals are her hips. Atala and the other lower worlds are her lower regions from her hip.

[35] The demigods began to behold her cosmic appearance with eyes wide awake, with wonder. Thousands of fiery rays emitted from her form. She began to kiss the whole universe with her lips.

[36] The two rows of teeth began to make horrible sounds. Fire came out from her eyes. The various weapons are seen in her hands. The 'Brahmin' and 'Kshatriya' became the food of that goddess.

[37] Thousands of heads, eyes and feet were seen in that form. Crores of suns, crores of lightning flashes, blazing everywhere.

[38] Horrible and awful, that appearance looked terrific to the eyes, heart and mind. The demigods thus began to utter cries of horror.

[39] Their hearts trembled and they were caught with stark fear. 'Here is the Devi, our mother and the Preserver'. This feeling vanished at once from their minds.

[40] The Vedas that were on the four sides of the Devi, with the tremendous sound, brought the demigods back to wakefulness who had fainted due to extreme fear.

[41] The demigods having patience, began to praise and chant hymns in words choked with tears of love flowing from their eyes.

[42] Demigods Said: O Mother! Forgive our faults. Protect us, because though miserable, we are born out of you.

[43] O Divine Mother! Withhold your anger. We are very much terrified at the sight of your form. O Devi! We are inferior immortals. What prayers can we offer to you!

[44] Your powers and forms cannot be comprehended even by the great sages. Then, how can it be understood by us!

[45] Salutations to you of the nature of the Pranava 'Om'. You are the one that is proved in all the Vedanta as the supreme. Salutation to you, the form of 'Hrim'!

[46] Salutations to you, the self of all, from whom the fire, the sun, and the moon have sprung. And all the medicinal plants have also sprung from you only.

[47] From you alone, all the demigods, animals, birds, and humans have arisen. Salutations to that self of all!

[48] We bow down again and again to your great form, Maha Maya, from whom have sprung the vital breath, grains and wheats, and who is the source of asceticism, faith, truth, continence and the rules about what to do and what not to do.

[49] The seven breaths, the seven worlds, the seven flames and the seven sacrifices have sprung from you only!

[50] Salutations to your universal form from whom have sprung all the oceans, all the mountains, all the rivers and all the plants.

[51] We bow down to your cosmic form from whom have originated the sacrifices, the donations, and the mantras of the Rig, the Yajur, and the Sama Vedas.

[52] O Mother! O Maha Maya! We bow down to your front, to your back, to your both sides, to your top, to your bottom and to all the sides.

[53] O Devi! Please withdraw this extraordinary terrific form of yours, and show us your kind and beautiful lovely form.

[54] Vyasa Said: Seeing the demigods so afraid, the world mother out of compassion withdrew her horrific form and showed her beautiful appearance, pleasing to the whole world.

[55] Her body became soft and gentle. In one hand she held the noose, and in another she held the goad. The two other hands made signs to dispel all fears and ready to grant the boons. Her eyes emitted rays of kindness and her face was adorned with beautiful smiles.

[56] Seeing that beautiful form of mother, the fear of the demigods dissolved completely. Their minds attained peace and overwhelmed with joy; they bowed down silently.

CHAPTER 04

YOGA OF KNOWLEDGE

[1] Shakti said: O Demigods! You are not at all worthy to see this wonderful cosmic form. But it is my affection towards the devotees that I have shown to you this great form of mine.

[2] The study of the Vedas, the yoga, the austerities, the sacrifice, or any other discipline are quite incompetent to make this form visible to anybody. Nobody can see this form without my grace.

[3] O King! Now hear the instructions carefully. The real self is the only supreme thing in this world of maya or illusion. The all-pervading Ishvara becomes an individual soul after assuming the doership.

[4] Then, the soul performs many acts leading to virtue and vice. It goes into various wombs and enjoys happiness or sorrow according to its actions.

[5] It remains involved constantly in many actions, due to which it attains various kinds of bodies, and experiences more happiness or sorrow indeed.

[6] Like a wheel that moves perpetually, the cycle of birth and death is endless. Ignorance alone is the root cause of this cycle. Desire comes out of ignorance and the action follows.

[7] A person should strive tirelessly to get rid of this ignorance. O Mountain King! The goal of life is obtained only when this ignorance is destroyed.

[8] The highest goal is attained by a Jiva, when it becomes liberated while living. And wisdom is the only thing that is able to destroy this mighty ignorance.

[9] As darkness cannot dispel darkness. Similarly, the action born out of ignorance is ignorance itself, and such an action cannot destroy ignorance. So, it is useless to expect that ignorance can be destroyed by doing various actions.

[10] The actions are totally futile because the Jivas want more and more sensual enjoyment out of their actions. Attachment arises out of this desire which leads to great calamity.

[11] The authentic scriptures declare that the final liberation comes from knowledge. So, one should try to live one hundred years acquiring knowledge.

[12] Therefore, every being should make best efforts to obtain that knowledge. And it is advised by scriptures to do actions that lead to knowledge. Hence, action and knowledge complement each other.

[13] But, some say that it is impossible. Since, the action and wisdom are contradictory.

[14] Coexistence of action and knowledge is not possible just as darkness and light cannot be brought together.

[15] Therefore, O King! Dedicate all your actions to me and work ceaselessly until the complete purification of the mind is achieved.

[16] The self-control and dispassion arise in purity. Hence, until that point is reached, you have to work. When you attain purity, the actions are not necessary.

[17] Once the purity of mind is achieved. The seeker must take refuge in a guru with complete devotion.

[18] One should day and night without any laziness, listen, think and deeply contemplate about Vedanta only.

[19] When the supreme self is realised, as a result the fearlessness arises and then you attain my eternal state.

[20] While studying Vedanta, you must understand the meaning of each word first, then the meaning of the sentence in its totality. If you practise in this manner, the knowledge of the eternal self is not very far away from you.

[21] The embodied soul or Jivatma and the supreme soul or Paramatma are one and the same. Only out of ignorance, they appear different.

[22] The wise see the unity of Jivatma and Paramatma. Although, the meaning of the two words is different. Therefore, the essence of the words must be taken according to the established scriptures.

[23] The essence of both the words is pure consciousness. Thus, they are one and the same. Realising this oneness, the individual soul transcends duality.

[24] The one who is freed from the gross and other bodies, attains oneness with the supreme self.

[25] The gross body arises from the five gross elements. It enjoys the fruits of its actions and is subject to old age, disease and death.

[26] This gross body is full of maya. Therefore, it is false, yet it appears as real. O Lord of Mountains! Know this to be my first limiting condition.

[27] The five sense organs, the five organs of action, five winds, mind and intellect, these seventeen combines to form the subtle body.

[28] This subtle body experiences pleasure and pain. Hence, this is my second limiting condition.

[29] Ignorance, without beginning and indescribable, is my third limiting condition. It appears as the causal body.

[30] When all these limiting conditions subside, only the supreme self remains. Within these three bodies (Gross, Subtle, Causal), the five bodily sheaths always exist.

[31] When the five sheaths are discarded using the 'neti neti' method, the true self is attained which is my real essence.

[32] The true self is neither born nor dies. It is not killed, even when the body is killed. It is unborn, eternal, and everlasting.

[33] If one wants to kill it and the other thinks that it can be killed, both of them do not know. The self can neither kill nor be killed.

[34] The self, subtler than the subtlest, and greater than the greatest, resides within the heart of every being. One who is free from desire and sorrow can only see the glory of the self.

[35] Know the self to be the owner, and the body to be the chariot. Know the mind to be the reins and the charioteer as the intellect.

[36] The senses being the horses. They stray from one object to another ceaselessly. The mind is the enjoyer.

[37] Those who are non-discriminating and always impure, do not realise the self, rather they are bound in this world.

[38] The one who is discriminating and always pure realises the self and from which there is no return.

[39] The one whose intellect as charioteer is wise, and who keeps his senses under control by keeping tight the reins of his mind. That one reaches my supreme state for sure.

[40] One should always meditate intensely on me to realise the nature of self by listening, thinking and contemplating.

[41] When by the constant practice, as mentioned above, one is fit for being absorbed in the self, just before that, one should understand the meanings of the separate letters in the seed mantra of maya.

[42] The seed mantra ‘Hrim’ has four matrikas or seeds; ‘Ha’, ‘Ra’, ‘Ee’ and ‘M’. The letter ‘Ha’ means gross body, the letter ‘Ra’ means subtle body and the letter ‘Ee’ means the causal body, and the ‘M’ is the fourth state.

[43] Thus meditating on the separate differentiated states, the intelligent one should meditate on the aforesaid three seeds in the cosmic body. And one should then try to establish relation between the whole, its parts and their unity.

[44] Before entering into the state of complete absorption, after carefully thinking the above, one should close one's eyes and meditate on me, the supreme ruler of the universe.

[45] O King! Putting a stop to all the worldly desires, one should equalise the inhalation and exhalation.

[46] With sincere devotion, one should dissolve the gross body denoted by the letter 'Ha' into 'Ra', the subtle body.

[47] Further, one should dissolve the subtle body denoted by 'Ra' into 'Ee', the causal body. One should then dissolve the causal body denoted by 'Ee' into 'M', the fourth state where there is no speech.

[48] The fourth state is absolutely free from all the dualities. It is of the form of existence, consciousness and bliss. Reflect upon it within the midst of the flame of consciousness.

[49] O King! By practising the above meditation, anyone can perceive me directly and become me only.

[50] Thus the firmly resolved intelligent person, by the practice of this yoga realises the self and immediately destroys the ignorance and all the actions.

CHAPTER 05

YOGA AND MANTRA

[1] Himavan said: O Mother! Now tell me about yoga with all its limbs giving the knowledge of the supreme consciousness so that I may realise the self, when I practise according to those instructions.

[2] Devi said: Yoga does not exist in the heavens, nor does it exist on earth or in the worlds below. Those who know say that the realisation of the unity of the Jivatma and the Paramatama is called ‘Yoga’.

[3] O Sinless One! The enemies to yoga are six and they are lust, anger, greed, attachment, pride and jealousy.

[4] The yogis break through the six enemies by practising the eight limbs of yoga.

[5] They are yama or restraint, niyama or observance, asana or correct-posture, pranayama or breath-control, pratyahara or withdrawal of senses, dharana or concentration, dhyana or meditation and samadhi or complete absorption.

[6] ‘Ahinsa’ or non-violence, ‘Satya’ or truthfulness, ‘Asteya’ or non-stealing, ‘Brahmacharya’ or continence, ‘Aparigraha’ or non-possessiveness, ‘Kshama’ or forgiveness, ‘Dhriti’ or fortitude, ‘Daya’

or compassion, ‘Arjava’ or honesty, and moderation in food & sleep, are the ten yama or restraints.

[7] Austerity, contentment, faith in God, charity, worship of God, studying vedic scriptures, humility, introspection, mantra chanting and fasting are the ten niyama or observances.

[8] There are five kinds of asanas or postures that are advisable; Padmasana, Svastikasana, Bhadrasana, Vajrasana and Virasana.

[9] Padmasan consists of crossing the legs and placing the feet on the opposite thighs and then sitting straight with ease.

[10] This posture is recommended by the yogis and by this one can raise oneself in the air.

[11] Place the soles of the feet completely under the thighs, keep the body straight, and sit at ease. This is called the Svastikasana.

[12] Bhadrasana consists in placing well the two heels on the two sides of the two nerves of the testicle, near the anus and catching by the two hands the two heels at the lower part of the testicles and then sitting at ease. This is very much liked by the yogis.

[13] Vajrasana consists in placing the feet on the two thighs respectively and placing the fingers below the thighs with the hands also there, and then sitting at ease.

[14] Virasana consists in sitting cross on the hams in placing the right foot under the right thigh and the left foot under the left thigh and sitting at ease with the body straight.

[15] Taking in the breath by the left nostril so long as we count 'Om' sixteen times.

[16] Hold the breath so long as we count 'Om' sixty-four times and then exhale it slowly by the right nostril as long as we count 'Om' thirty-two times.

[17] The first process of inhalation is called 'Puraka', the second process of holding is called 'Kumbhaka', and the third process of exhalation is called 'Rechaka'. This complete process is called pranayama by those versed in yoga.

[18] Thus one should again repeat the processes in the same order. In the beginning, try with the number twelve as we count 'Om' twelve times and then increase the number gradually to sixteen.

[19] Pranayama is of two kinds; Sagarbha and Vigarbha. It is called Sagarbha when Pranayama is performed with chanting mantras or meditation. It is called Vigarbha Pranayama when 'Om' is simply counted and no other mantra.

[20] When pranayama is practised repeatedly, perspiration comes first when it is of the lowest stage; when the body begins to tremble, it is

called middling; and when one rises up in the air, leaving the ground, it is called the best pranayama.

[21] The senses travel spontaneously towards their objects, as if they are without anyone to check.

[22] To curb the senses and to make them turn backwards from those objects is called pratyahara.

[23] To hold the vital breath on toes, heels, knees, thighs, genital organs, navel, heart, throat, the soft palate, nose, between the eyebrows, and on the top of the head, at these twelve places respectively is called dharana or concentration.

[24] Focus the mind on the consciousness inside and then meditate on the deity. This is called dhyana or meditation.

[25] Samadhi is the state of complete absorption in which there is no difference between Jivatma and Paramatama.

[26] O King! Thus, I have described to you in detail about all the eight limbs of yoga.

[27] This body is composed of the five elements, which is the essence of the sun, the moon, and the stars.

[28] There are 350,000 nerves in this body; out of which the principal is ten. Out of ten again, three are most prominent.

[29] The foremost of these three is ‘Susumna’ situated in the centre of the spinal cord.

[30] On the left of this is the ‘Ida’ of the nature of a female, representing the moon. While, on the right side is the ‘Pingala’ of the nature of a male, representing the sun.

[31] There is a cobweb like formation in the innermost area of Sushumna, called ‘Vichitra’ or ‘Chitrini Bhulinga’, the centre of which is the seat of will, knowledge, and action.

[32] Inside the ‘Vichitra’ is the svayambhu-linga, like a crore of suns it shines! Above that is the seed mantra of maya, the form of ‘Ha’, ‘Ra’, ‘Ee’ and nasal ‘M’.

[33] Above that is a red coloured, ‘Kundalini’, appearing like a flame. It is declared to be my essence.

[34] Outside it is the four-petaled lotus of a yellow colour comprising the four letters ‘va’, ‘sa’, ‘sha’, and ‘scha’. The yogis meditate on this. In its centre is the hexagonal space. This is called the ‘Muladhara Chakra’ for it is the base and it supports all the six lotuses.

[35] Above it is the ‘Svadhisthana Chakra’, emitting lustre like diamond and with six petals representing the six letters ‘ba’, ‘bha’, ‘ma’, ‘ya’, ‘ra’, ‘la’.

[36] The word ‘Sva’ means supreme linga or superior male symbol. Therefore, the sages call this ‘Svadhisthana Chakra’.

[37] Above it, is situated the ‘Manipura Chakra’ of the colour of lightning in clouds and very fiery. It comprises the ten petals representing the ten letters ‘ḍa’, ‘ḍha’, ‘ṇa’, ‘ta’, ‘tha’, ‘da’, ‘dha’, ‘na’, ‘pa’, ‘pha’.

[38] The lotus resembles a full-blown pearl. Hence, it is ‘Manipadma’. Vishnu dwells here. Meditation here leads to the sight of Vishnu.

[39] Above it is ‘Anahata Chakra’ with the twelve petals representing, the twelve letters ‘ka’, ‘kha’, ‘ga’, ‘gha’, ‘ṅa’, ‘ca’, ‘cha’, ‘ja’, ‘jha’, ‘ña’, ‘ṭa’, ‘ṭha’.

[40] In the middle is Banalinga, shining like a thousand suns. This lotus emits the sound without being struck.

[41] This is the source of all joy. Here dwells the Rudra, the supreme person. It is highly renowned among the sages.

[42] Above it is situated the ‘Vishuddha Chakra’ of the sixteen petals, comprising the sixteen letters ‘a’, ‘ā’, ‘i’, ‘ī’, ‘u’, ‘ū’, ‘ṛ’, ‘ṝ’, ‘ḷ’, ‘ḹ’, ‘e’, ‘ai’, ‘o’, ‘au’, ‘aṃ’, ‘aḥ’.

[43] This is of a smoky colour, highly lustrous, and is situated in the throat. The Jivatma sees the Paramatma here and it gets purified, hence

this chakra is called ‘Vishuddha’. This wonderful lotus is termed as ‘Akasha’ as well.

[44] Above that is situated, between the eyebrows, the exceedingly beautiful ‘Ajña Chakra’ with two petals comprising the two letters ‘ha’ and ‘ksha’.

[45] The self resides in this lotus. When people are situated here, they can see everything and know of the present, past and future. One gets the commands from the divine, therefore it is called the ‘Ajña Chakra’.

[46] Above that is the ‘Kailasha Chakra’ and above it too is the ‘Rodhini Chakra’. These supporting chakras have been described by me for advanced yogis.

[47] The prominent yogis say that above that again, is the seat of the supreme deity with thousand petals. O King! Thus, I have declared the best of the paths leading to yoga.

[48] First, by ‘Puraka’ pranayama, fix the mind on ‘Muladhara Chakra’. Then, contract and arouse the kundalini shakti by that air between the anus and genital organ.

[49] One should attain the highest point by piercing the lingas in various chakras all the way to the thousand petalled lotus at the crown of the head. Then meditate on the Shakti united with Shambhu there.

[50] Out of the meeting of Shiva and Shakti, a kind of nectar is produced. That nectar of joy, the wise yogis offer to maya to drink, in exchange for yielding success in yoga.

[51] After pleasing all the gods in the six chakras with the offerings of that nectar, the yogi brings the shakti down again on the muladhara.

[52] Thus by daily practising this, all the above mantras will no doubt, be made to come to complete success.

[53] One will be freed from the bondage of the world, filled with old age, death and other miseries.

[54] O Child! The practice of breath control is most important. There is no doubt in this. I have described to you the most excellent yoga.

[55] Now hear from me the dharana yoga. To fix thoroughly one's mind on the supreme light of mine, transcending space and time, leads soon to the union of the Jiva and Paramatama.

[56] If one does not succeed in yoga, owing to impurities of the mind, then the yogi must adopt what is called the 'Avayava Yoga'.

[57] O King! The devotees should fix the mind on my gentle hands, feet and other limbs one by one and try to master each of these places.

[58] Thereby the mind would be purified. Then one should fix that purified mind on my whole body.

[59] The yogis must practise with mantras till the mind is not dissolved in me, or my consciousness.

[60] By the practice of meditating on mantras, the thing to be known by Vedas is transformed into knowledge. Know this as certain, that mantras are futile without yoga and the yoga is futile without mantras. The mantra and the yoga are the two infallible means to realise the eternal self.

[61] As a jar surrounded by darkness in the room is visible by means of a lamp, so this Paramatma, surrounded by maya, is visible to the Jiva by means of mantra.

[62] O Mountain King! Thus, I have described to you the yoga with their limbs.

[63] You should receive the teachings about them from the mouth of a guru or else millions of scriptures will never be able to give you a true realisation of self.

CHAPTER 06

KNOWLEDGE OF SELF

[1] Shakti said: O Himavan! Assuming a comfortable posture with devotion that is completely sincere, one should meditate on my nature.

[2] That is manifest and near. Also, pervading in the hearts of all beings. It is the well-known highest goal. Whatever waking, dreaming, or sleeping, breathing or blinking is done, all happens within me.

[3] It is beyond being and non-being, higher than wisdom. It is the best adoration for all creatures. It is smaller than the smallest and yet, the foundation of all the worlds.

[4] It is the imperishable 'Brahman'. It is the creator, the revealer of sacred knowledge and the cosmic mind. It is real and immortal. O Gentle One! Know that it is the sole goal of the entire creation.

[5] Taking the bow of the scriptures, the arrow of the mind; sharpened by concentration, drawing it with the target as the imperishable self.

[6] The target is hit by only those, who are always immersed in listening, thinking and contemplating about the self.

[7] Know it to be the one support of all. Discard all other thoughts, since it is the only refuge for the mortals.

[8] Where all the 72,000 nerves come together, as the spokes in a wheel, that is the place of the eternal soul.

[9] Meditate on the eternal self as ‘Om’ with all its attributes, in order to acquire the knowledge of the Paramatma, who is beyond the darkness and also, who is self-luminous. Your welfare will be ensured only by such knowledge.

[10] The all-knowing self is to be meditated upon as the controller of the mind and the guide of the senses. When it manifests itself as existence and bliss, it is experienced only by the wise through the purity of mind.

[11] All doubts are completely removed and all fruits of past action are destroyed, when the transcendental self is realised.

[12] The Brahman, pure and indivisible, is the highest truth. The knowers of the self, claim it to be the light of the lights.

[13] The sun does not shine nor the moon and the stars shine in its absence. When it shines everything shines, by its light everything becomes manifest.

[14] This self alone is immortal. It pervades all the directions; front and behind, right and left, above and below.

[15] The one who is completely merged in Brahman is always satisfied and is considered the best among all. That person never grieves nor desires anything.

[16] O Mountain King! There is a great fear in duality. The fear arises from the idea of a second. Where there is no second, the fear ceases to exist. Since I am not separate from the self, the self is also not separate from me.

[17] O Himavan! Know that I am the eternal self. The vision of me is possible only there, where my devotees chant my prayers and wise ones abide in my essence.

[18] Neither I dwell in any sacred place of pilgrimage, nor do I live in 'Kailasha' nor in 'Vaikuntha' nor in any other place. I reside in the lotus heart of my devotees.

[19] The blessed person, who worships me even once, by knowing my true essence, that gets a crore times the fruit of worshipping me. That one's mother becomes blessed and the whole family is rendered pure.

[20] O Himavan! I have now told everything that you asked about 'Brahma Jñana'. Now, nothing remains to be described further. The one whose heart is completely merged in the all-pervading consciousness purifies the whole world. There is no doubt in this.

[21] This knowledge should be imparted to only those who are of good character, well versed in the scriptures and completely devoted to me. This should not be given to any other type of person.

[22] The one who is fully devoted to his personal deity and who is equally devoted to his guru, to those persons only this knowledge should be declared.

[23] Verily, that is the god itself, who advises this knowledge to others. No one is able to repay the debts of such a guru.

[24] The scriptures rank the guru higher than the parents, since the birth given by the parents is perishable while the birth given by the guru is eternal and imperishable.

[25] The scriptures conclude that the guru who gives the knowledge of the self is supreme.

[26] Since, when the god is angered, the guru can protect. But, when the guru is angered, even the god cannot save us. Hence, the guru should be served with the utmost devotion.

[27] The guru must be served by body, mind, and word. One should always try to please the guru in all possible manner. Otherwise, if a guru becomes unmerciful, then certainly no one can save you in all the three worlds.

[28] O Himavan! It is very difficult to acquire 'Brahma Jñana'. Hear a story now. A saint named 'Dadhyarna' of the Atharvana family went to Indra and prayed to him to give the knowledge of self.

[29] Indra Said: I would give you eternal knowledge, but if you impart it to anybody, I would sever your head. He agreed to this and Indra gave him the highest knowledge.

[30] After a few days, the two Ashvins came to him and prayed for that knowledge. He humbly turned down their request by saying that his head would be cut off, if he disclosed this knowledge to anyone.

[31] Ashvins Said: We will cut your head now and keep it elsewhere and we will attach the head of a horse to your body. Instruct us with the mouth of this horse and when Indra will cut off your head, we will place your former head.

[32] The saint, pleased with their intellect, gave them the highest knowledge. Indra cut off his head by his thunderbolt. When the horse-head of the saint was cut off, the two physicians replaced it with his original head. This story is widely known in all the Vedas.

CHAPTER 07

YOGA OF DEVOTION

[1] O Divine Mother! Now describe the yoga of devotion to me, by which even an ordinary person having no dispassion reaches the knowledge of self easily.

[2] Devi said: O Mountain King! There are three paths, widely known, leading to liberation. These are 'Karma Yoga' or the path of action, 'Jñana Yoga' or the path of knowledge and 'Bhakti Yoga' or the path of devotion.

[3] Of these three paths, the path of devotion is most suitable because people can practise this continually by bringing their minds to concentration, without any suffering to the body.

[4] This devotion again is of three kinds as there are three gunas. They are 'Tamasik', 'Rajasik' and 'Sattvik'.

[5] The one who worships me, to cause harm to others, being filled with ego, jealousy and anger is called tamasik devotion.

[6] When one worships me for one's own desires and does not intend to do harm to others, this is called rajasik devotion.

[7] The rajasik devotees, forever filled with desires, desirous of fame and money, and thinking themselves to be different from me, worship me with great devotion.

[8] When people worship me to purify their sins, knowing that their actions are authorised by ten niyama or observances and therefore must be performed, also offer to me the results of all their actions. This is called sattvik devotion.

[9] The sattvik devotees, thinking themselves to be separate from me, perform all their actions for the sake of my love.

[10] The sattvik devotion leads to supreme devotion. The rajasik and tamasik devotion do not lead to supreme devotion, since they are tainted by selfishness.

[11] Now hear attentively about the supreme devotion that I am describing to you.

[12] Those who always hear my glories and chant my names, for them, all the auspicious qualities flow steadily into them, as a stream of oil flows steadily into a vessel.

[13] Those who do not want the fruit of their actions, and seek no liberation. They have no motive at all.

[14] They are filled with devotion for me only, worship me alone, and know nothing other than me to serve. They are least interested in final liberation even.

[15] They think about me tirelessly with utmost devotion. Knowing me as not separate from themselves. They are my supreme devotees.

[16] They consider all the Jivas as myself and love me as oneself. They do not make any difference between the Jivas and myself as they find the same consciousness everywhere and manifested in all.

[17] They do not quarrel with anybody as they have abandoned all ideas about separateness.

[18] They bow down and worship from the lowest beings to the supreme one. They never wish to cause harm to another.

[19] They become filled with devotion whenever they see my sacred places, my devotees, hear the scriptures describing my deeds and whenever they meditate on my mantras.

[20] They get goosebumps overwhelmed with love for me and tears of love flow incessantly from their eyes. They chant my names and my deeds in a voice, choked with the feelings of love for me.

[21] O King! They worship me as the mother of the whole universe and the cause of all the causes.

[22] They perform the daily and occasional duties and all my vows and sacrifices without showing any miserly feeling in their expenditure.

[23] They naturally long to perform my festivities and to visit places where my festivals are held.

[24] They sing my names loudly and dance, being intoxicated with my love, and have no idea of egoism and are devoid of the body feeling.

[25] They think that according to the law of karma, whatever are the results of their past actions, would surely manifest without a doubt.

[26] Therefore, they should not be much worried about the future and focus on their present actions. This type of devotion is called the supreme devotion indeed.

[27] The person whose heart is filled with the supreme devotion, that one would get immediately dissolved in my nature of consciousness.

[28] The sages call this stage of consciousness as wisdom. When this wisdom arises, devotion and dispassion get their ends satisfied.

[29] When the sense of ego does not crop up by one's past actions, although that person has not given up the fruits of one's actions. Then, knowledge of me may not arise, but that person goes to my abode because of devotion to me.

[30] That person enjoys there, all the objects of enjoyment, and at the end attains to my knowledge, by that attains to the final liberation forever. Without my knowledge, the final liberation is impossible.

[31] O Himavan! The one who has realised the eternal self, after leaving the body, does not take re-birth.

[32] The scriptures state that the one who has realised the self becomes that eternal self.

[33] Out of ignorance, as one searches for the cap, which is already on the head. Similarly, one searches for the self, which is already oneself.

[34] O Mountain King! My form is different from the known and the unknown. The image of the self is seen in the bodies as the image falls in a mirror. As the image falls in water, so that self is seen in the world of departed ancestors.

[35] As the difference between shadow and light is absolutely clear, so in my abode, the knowledge that arises out of oneness is absolute and devoid of duality.

[36] The one who leaves this body without attaining wisdom, although that person was dispassionate and practised yoga regularly, resides in the Brahmaloka for a very long period.

[37] Then that person takes birth in a pure hearted, prosperous family and again practising yoga, finally gets my knowledge.

[38] O King! This wisdom arises after many births, it does not come in one birth. So, one should try one's best to get this knowledge. If, attaining this rare human birth, one does not strive for this knowledge. Know that a great misfortune has befallen to that person.

[39] For this human birth is very hard to attain and then the birth in a 'Brahmin' family is rarer, moreover among the brahmins as well, the knowledge of the Vedas is very rare.

[40] The attaining of the six virtues; tranquillity, control of the senses, contentment, endurance, faith and a burning desire for liberation; the acquisition of a real guru and the success in yoga, all these are very hard to be attained in this life.

[41] The desire for the final liberation takes birth in only those, who have acquired merits in the past crores of births.

[42] That person's birth is entirely a waste, who even after gaining all the above virtues, does not try his best to attain this eternal knowledge.

[43] Hence, one should try one's best to acquire this wisdom. Thus, at every moment, that person gets the fruits of the Ashvamedha sacrifice. There is no doubt in this.

[44] As 'Ghee' or clarified butter resides hidden in the milk, so this knowledge resides hidden in everybody. With the mind as a churning rod, the churning should be done tirelessly. Hence slowly, the knowledge of the imperishable 'Brahman' would be attained.

[45] Having attained this eternal wisdom, one is absolutely fulfilled. The Vedanta has proclaimed this very loud and clear.

[46] O King! Thus, I have described to you all that you wanted to hear. Now what more do you want!

9 798888 692141

Printed by Libri Plureos GmbH in Hamburg,
Germany